ISBN: 979-8-218-25979-2 (paperback)

Russian Cursive Writing for Kids and Adults is a practical textbook for students who want to learn Russian cursive script or transition from writing in block letters to cursive writing. It has been tested in a classroom with kids and adult learners, and can also be used by anyone who wants to improve their Russian cursive writing. It offers step-by-step and easy to follow instructions with examples, teaches how to connect letters for efficient writing, and introduces fun facts and practical information.

The current edition is suitable for students of all levels of Russian.

Three main ways to connect Russian cursive letters

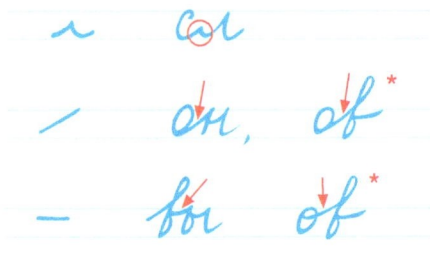

*Choose the option that fits your handwriting style

In cursive writing, we need connections to bring a hand/a pen/a pencil or whatever you are writing with to a position where the next letter starts. Many Russian cursive letters have «tails» that we will use as connections.

Let's write the word «слон»

Слон = 4 letters

1.   **С** *C*

2.   **Л** Л starts low _____ . Therefore, we need a low connection _____ .

3.   **О** О starts at the top here _____ , so here's how we write it in a word _____ .
Remember to go down _____ and circle it an extra time _____ to connect to the next letter _____ .

4.   **Н** Н starts at the top, so we bring the connection to the top _____

Here's our word _____

Please note that your parents or teacher might have a different handwriting style and therefore might connect letters differently. Below are examples of handwriting of different people who went to school at different times.

Экономические отношения
между людьми

Экономический интерес —
побудительный мотив,
стимул человеческой
хозяйственной деятельности
в каком - либо направ-
лении.
Экономический закон —
объективно необходимые.

О, как же я хочу,
Нечуемый никем,
Лететь вослед лучу,
Где нет меня совсем.

А ты в кругу лучись, —
Другого счастья нет —
И у звезды учись
Тому, что значит свет.

Жил да был карась
Вот и сказка началась
Жили были два налима,
Вот и сказки половина.
Жили были три гуся,
Вот и сказка вся.

Люблю тебя, Петра творенье,
Люблю твой строгий, стройный вид,
Невы державное теченье,
Береговой её гранит,
Твоих оград узор чугунный,
Твоих задумчивых ночей
Прозрачный сумрак,
            блеск безлунный,
Когда я в комнате моей
Пишу, читаю без лампады,
И ясны спящие громады
Пустынных улиц, и светла
Адмиралтейская игла,
И, не пуская тьму ночную
На золотые небеса,
Одна заря сменить другую
Спешит, дав ночи полчаса.

Люда
Иди всегда вперёд!
И ни, шагу назад.

Таня

Color-coded strokes and connections

When I teach Russian cursive writing, I often use colored pens to show connections and the sequence of strokes. In this textbook blue is the main color. If a letter or a word should be written in one stroke it appears in blue.

For example, Ж, дом

ж, дом

If a letter or a word is written in two or more strokes, each stroke or connection appears in a different color. In this textbook I use **red** and **purple** in addition to blue. Feel free to use the colors you like.

For examples, флаг, кот. Я живу в Москве.

флаг кот
Я живу в Москве.

Incline

Russian cursive writing is slightly inclined to the right.

Я живу в Москве.

This is a chapter book

In this textbook all letters are sorted by common elements. There are six chapters. Each chapter contains letters with one element in common, or several sets of letters that together have a common element or elements. I encourage you to use the blank lines and pages for additional practice. In the last chapter you will find exercises to test how well you can write and read Russian cursive writing.

I hope this little textbook will help you to master Russian cursive writing and will make learning easy and fun.

$C\ c\quad C\ c$

$Cc\ Cc\ Cc\ Cc\ Cc\ Cc\ Cc\ Cc$

$C\ c$

$Э\ э\quad Ɔ\ _1\quad Э\ _2\quad э$

$Ээ\ Ээ\ Ээ\ Ээ\ Ээ\ Ээ\ Ээ$

$Э\ э$

$X\ x\quad Ɔ\ _1\quad X\ _2\ x\quad Ɔ + C = X$

$Xx\ Xx\ Xx\ Xx\ Xx\ Xx$

$X\ x$

$O\ o\quad O\ o\qquad O + \tfrac{1}{2}\ C = o$

$Oo\ Oo\ Oo\ Oo\ Oo\ Oo\ Oo$

$O\ o$

$Co\ co\quad Co^2\quad Co$

$Co\ co\quad Co\ co\quad Co\ co$

$Co\ co$

$Эс\ эс\quad эс$

$Эс\ эс\ Эс\ эс\ Эс\ эс\ Эс\ эс$

$Эс\ эс$

Ж ж   Э У И И Ж   Э + / + С = Ж   Ж

Ж ж   Ж ж   Ж ж   Ж ж   Ж ж

Ж ж   Ж ж   Ж ж   Ж ж

ож   ОЖ

$$\mathscr{N}_{1} + \mathscr{A}_{2} = \mathscr{A} \quad o_{1} \quad a_{2}$$

Аа Аа Аа А Аа

А а

л л л л

Л л Л л Л л Л л Л л

Л л

М м М м

М м М м М м М м x

М м

Ии Ии Ий Ий

Ии Ии Ии Ии Ии Ии

И и , й

ил   *Ли*   *ии*

Ил   *ии*   *Ии*

ма   *ам*   *ма*

а   *Алла*

а   *Мила*

Ц Ц + ᵭ = Ц   ᵭ   Ц

Ц ц   Ц ц   Ц ц   Ц ц   Ц ц

Ш ш   Ш ш   Ш ш   **optional**   ш

Ш ш   Ш ш   Ш ш   Ш ш

Ш ш

Щ щ   Щ + ᵭ = Щ

Щ щ   Щ щ   Щ щ   Щ щ   Щ щ

Щ щ

цо   иц
                       иц

ши   ши   ши

иши   иши   иши   и ш и

лицо   лицо   л и ц о

Миша   Миша   М и ш а

жу

уж

У у У у

У у

Ч ч Ч ч

Ч ч

ы ы ы ы

ь ь ь ь

ъ ъ ъ ъ

мы

уши, у_ши

ищи

ча   чу

часы

соль

съ

Я я   *Я*   *Я*   *я*   Я

Я я   *Я я*   *Я я*   *Я я*   *Я я*   *Я я*   *Я я*

Я я

ия   ия

ля   ля

мя   мя

ая   ая

Я

$Tг$ $| $ + $⌐$ = T

$Tг$ $Tг$ $Tг$ $Tг$ $Tг$ $Tг$

$Tг$

$Пп$ $| $ ll $П$ $| $ + l + $⌐$ = $П$

n $| $ + $г$ = n

$Пп$ $Пп$ $Пп$ $Пп$ $Пп$

$Пп$

$Тт$ ll l $Т$

m $| $ + n = m

$Тт$ $Тт$ $Тт$ $Тт$

$Тт$

па | $го$ $па$

на | $папа$ $папа$

Pp p $| $ P $|p$ $| $ + p = p p $| $ + $г$ = p

Pp p Pp p Pp p Pp p

Pp, p

р | $тигр$ $тигр$

ма | $Рома$ $Рома$

*Choose the option that works best for you.

по, то, го	по, то,
пи, ти, ги	пи, ти,
ого	ого
пото́м	пото́м
потому что	потому
при, при	при
Ри́та	Ри́та
торт, торт	торт
то́рты то́рты	то́рты
мост	мост
холм	холм

Ф

фл

флаг

К

$\mathcal{K}$ $\mathcal{K}$ κ $\mathcal{K}$ $\mathcal{K}$ $\mathcal{K}$ + r = $\mathcal{K}$

κ r κ r + = κ

$\mathcal{K}$, $\mathcal{K}$ κ $\mathcal{K}$, $\mathcal{K}$ κ $\mathcal{K}$, $\mathcal{K}$ κ $\mathcal{K}$, $\mathcal{K}$ κ

$\mathcal{K}$ $\mathcal{K}$ κ

Н

$\mathcal{H}$, $\mathcal{H}$ κ $\mathcal{H}$ $\mathcal{J}$ $\mathcal{H}$ $\mathcal{H}$

$н$ $н$ $нн$ $н$

$\mathcal{H}$ $\mathcal{H}$ $н$ $\mathcal{H}$, $\mathcal{H}$ $н$ $\mathcal{H}$, $\mathcal{H}$ $н$

$\mathcal{H}$, $\mathcal{H}$ $н$

кн

$кн$ $кн$ $кн$ $кн$ $кн$

ук

$ук$ $ук$

на, ▮

$на$ $но$

нога

$нога$

кот

$кот$

Нин▮

$Нина$

Ю

$\mathcal{HO}$, $\mathcal{HO}$ $ю$ $\mathcal{J}$ $\mathcal{HO}$ $\mathcal{J}$ + $о$ = $\mathcal{HO}$ r $ю$ r + $о$ = $ю$

$\mathcal{HO}$, $\mathcal{HO}$ $ю$ $\mathcal{HO}$, $\mathcal{HO}$ $ю$ $\mathcal{HO}$, $\mathcal{HO}$ $ю$ $\mathcal{HO}$, $\mathcal{HO}$ $ю$

$\mathcal{HO}$, $\mathcal{HO}$ $ю$

юг

$юг$

*Choose the option that works best for you.

З з   З з   ᴣ   З   ᴣ
₁   ₂

З з   З з   З з   З з   З з   З з

З з

Є е   Є   С   Є е   ᴠ   е
₁   ₂

Ё ё   Ё   Ё   е ё
₁   ₁   ²   ²

Ё е   Ё ё

ёл   ёл

сье

Д д   ʃ   Д   д д
₁   ₂

Д д   Д д   Д д   Д д   Д д

Д д

Б б   ʃ   ᴆ   Б   с ᴆ   б
₁   ²

Б б   Б б   Б б   Б б   Б б

Б б

В в   ʃ   ᴦ   В   ᴠ в в

В в   В в   В в   В в   В в

В в

, ёл

е

Бо   ь   Б   Бо

ба

Вы   Вы

дом

Дима

Вова

ёлка

лёд

баба

Борис, Борис

	Бо
	ба
	Вы
	дом
	Ди́м
	Во́в
	ёлк
	лёд
	ба́б
	Бор

С с   *С с*

Э э   *Э э*

Х х   *Х х*

Ж ж   *Ж ж*

О о   *О о*

Л л   *Л л*

М м   *М м*

А а   *А а*

И и й   *И и й*

Ц ц   *Ц ц*

Ш ш   *Ш ш*

Щ щ   *Щ щ*

У у   *У у*

Ч ч   *Ч ч*

Д д   *Д д*

Б б   *Б б*

В в   *В в*

Я я   *Я я*

Г г Г г г

П п П п п

Т т Т т т

Р р Р р, р

Ф ф Ф ф

К к К к к

Н н Н н н

Ю ю Ю ю ю

З з З з

Е е Е е

Ё ё Ё ё

ы ы

ъ ъ

ь ь

двор двор двор шхуна шхуна

флаг флаг ёжик ёжик

Юля Юля хобот хобот

часы часы заяц заяц

Я живу в Москве.

Let's practice writing birthday and holiday greetings in Russian.

If you want to say «Happy Birthday!» or «Happy New Year!» in Russian, you will literally say «I/we congratulate you with birthday/New Year!» Pronouns «я» and «мы» are usually omitted as the verb form conveys whether it is singular or plural.

Поздравлять – to congratulate

Present tense

я (I) поздравляю	мы (we) поздравляем
ты (you) поздравляешь	вы/Вы (*you) поздравляете
он, она (he, she) поздравляет	они (they) поздравляют

*вы-you, plural; Вы -you, singular, formal

Merry Christmas and Happy New Year!

If the recipient of your message celebrates Christmas after the New Year, you should say «Поздравляю с Новым годом и Рождеством!»

Поздравляю с Рождеством и Новым годом!

Поздравляю с Новым годом и Рождеством!

Happy New Year to you!

[я] *Поздравляю тебя с Новым годом!*

*тебя is a form of you in genitive & accusative cases. You can replace «тебя» with «вас/Вас»

Happy Birthday to you!

[мы] *Поздравляем тебя с днём рождения!*

Желать – to wish

Present tense

я (I) желаю	мы (we) желаем
ты (you) желаешь	вы/Вы (you) желаете
он, она (he, she) желает	они (they) желают

It is customary to add a wish to a greeting. For example, you can wish health, happiness, or luck.

Wishing you health and happiness!

[я] *Желаю здоровья и счастья!*

[мы] *Желаем (тебе, вам, Вам) здоровья и счастья!*

Create your own birthday or a holiday greeting from the words below.

1	2	3
поздраваляю	тебя, вас, Вас	с Рождеством
поздравляем		с Новым годом
		с днём рождения
желаю	тебе, вам, Вам	здоровья
желаем		счастья
		удачи (luck)

So now you are an expert in cursive writing. Did you know that for some people studying and analyzing cursive writing is a profession?

Handwriting experts

There are areas of forensic expertise that deal with the authenticity of handwritten documents. Forensic handwriting experts are specialists that examine such documents and confirm if the handwriting is that of a specific person. Every person has a unique handwriting style. Among other things, forensic handwriting experts can tell whether a person:

• wrote a note in a hurry

• is right-or left-handed

• is native to a country or a foreigner

• is pretending to be someone else

A forensic handwriting expert can collect a lot of other information by analyzing handwriting. This information can be used to help police catch a criminal, to authenticate historic or literary documents and signatures, and to protect kids whose handwriting was used for criminal purposes. In Russia there are still many documents that must be handwritten or signed by a person. Conclusions of a professional forensic handwriting expert are admissible in the courts of many countries, including Russia.

Now you can write in Russian.
I'd love to see how you are doing! Please email me a sample of your handwriting.
My email is lmforeignlanguagematerials@gmail.com

Желаю успеха!

www.ingramcontent.com/pod-product-compliance
Lightning Source LLC
Chambersburg PA
CBHW041645120626
46547CB00017B/2624